English Olympiad

Book 1

www.pegasusforkids.com

© **B. Jain Publishers (P) Ltd.** All rights reserved. No part of this book may be reproduced, stored in a retrieval system or transmitted, in any form or by any means, mechanical, photocopying, recording or otherwise, without any prior written permission of the publisher.

Published by Kuldeep Jain for B. Jain Publishers (P) Ltd., D-157, Sector 63, Noida - 201307, U.P.

Registered office: 1921/10, Chuna Mandi, Paharganj, New Delhi-110055

Printed in India at Narain Printers & Binder, Noida

Preface

English Olympiad Book–1 has been carefully written, designed and brought to fruition keeping in mind the requirements of the students. It has almost all necessary elements that make each exercise a learning experience for the children, their teachers and parents.

'Learning by doing' – the ethos behind introducing Olympiads is an effort to achieve perfection. In this spirit, we have followed a systematic pattern, inclusive of the scientific method and child-centric approach, wherein each concept has been explained again (as understood that it was done as part of grammar lessons). Therefore, revisions here leave enough room to substantiate upon experiential learning that help students to deliver better.

In the end of the book, we have also provided three test papers that carry a diverse set of questions. It will help children test themselves amidst all concepts put together in random order, which will bring greater degree of clarity and thought.

Salient Features

- Multiple choice questions
- Use of necessary illustrations to make learning simpler
- Model test papers in the end to make a wholesome assessment
- Inclusion of almost all aspects of English Olympiad exams

We wish all readers of **English Olympiad Book–1** a joyful experience.

Contents

1. Jumbled Words 5
2. Identify Words from Pictures 8
3. Word Pairs/Odd One Out 11
4. Words and Their Meanings 14
5. Opposites 17
6. Nouns 19
7. One and Many 23
8. Gender 26
9. Pronouns 30
10. Using A, An and The 34
11. Action Words 37
12. Prepositions 40
13. Describing Words 43
14. People and Professions/Young Ones 46
15. Comprehension 49
    Model Test Paper-1 53
    Model Test Paper-2 56
    Model Test Paper-3 60
Answer Key 63

Jumbled Words

Look at this word: ICNE

Do you think it makes any sense?

Let us rearrange the letters to make it meaningful: **NICE**

Here, **ICNE** is a jumbled word. When the letters of a word are not in correct order, it is called a jumbled word.

We must rearrange jumbled letters of a word to make it meaningful.

Isn't that interesting? Now let's do some more.

EXERCISE 1

Solve these jumbled words. There is only one correct answer for each. Circle it.

1. **SENW**
   a) SNEW   b) WENS   c) ENSW   d) NEWS

2. **RCAWL**
   a) LWARC   b) RAWLC   c) CRAWL   d) AWRLC

3. **REVBA**
   a) EVBRA   b) BRAVE   c) VEBRA   d) RABVE

4. **TEKCIT**
   a) KETTIC   b) TICKET   c) CITKET   d) TICETK

5. **IKET**
   a) KITE   b) TEIK   c) TEKI   d) IKTE

6. **LEFA**
   a) AFEL b) EFAL c) LEAF d) FLAE

7. **LNUCH**
   a) NUCLH b) LCNUH c) NCHUL d) LUNCH

8. **BORWN**
   a) BROWN b) NBROW c) BOWRN d) ROWNBO

9. **PATORR**
   a) PATRRO b) PARROT c) PRROTA d) PRORTA

10. **PMEO**
    a) PMOE b) PEOM c) POEM d) MEOP

EXERCISE 2

Alisha arranged stickers of letters to paste on her notebooks and books of every subject. Her dog Leo jumbled those up. Can you help Alisha with the correct spellings?

1. **ECSCIEN**
   a) ECSCINE b) SCIENCE c) ENSW d) NEWS

2. **THAM**
   a) HAMT b) AMTH c) MATH d) TAMH

3. **DERREA**
   a) READER b) READRE c) AREDRE d) DRREAE

4. **LISHENG**
   a) ENGSHLI b) ENGLISH c) LISHGNE d) ENGSHIL

5. **DIHIN**
a) HINID b) HIIND c) HINDI d) DINIH

6. **WINGDRA**
a) DRAWING b) DRAWGNI c) GNIDRAW d) DRAWNGI

7. **INGCOLOUR**
a) COLOURGNI b) COLOURING c) GNILOURCO d) LOUROCGNI

8. **MMARGRA**
a) GRAMARM b) MARGARM c) GRAMMAR d) MRAGMAR

9. **BOOKWORK**
a) WORKBOOK b) KROWKOOB c) BOOKROWK d) ROWKOOKB

10. **WORKMOEH**
a) WORKHOME b) HOMEROWK c) EMOHWORK d) HOMEWORK

Identify Words from Pictures

EXERCISE 1

Identify the pictures and tick (✓) the correct answers.

1. a) telephone   b) keys
   c) tool   d) hairclip

2. a) window   b) door
   c) dancer   d) balloon

3. a) cartoon   b) dog
   c) cat   d) rat

4. a) calendar   b) notebook
   c) book   d) diary

5. a) school bus   b) tram
   c) truck   d) train

6. a) shirt   b) flag
   c) flower   d) emblem

7. a) drums   b) piano
   c) harmonica   d) tabla

8. a) rose   b) sunflower
    c) tulip   d) lotus

9. a) cub   b) calf
    c) puppy   d) kitten

10. a) doctor   b) sportsman
    c) policeman   d) postman

EXERCISE 2

Look at the pictures and choose the correct options to fill in the blanks.

1. **This _____ is made of mud and straw.**
   a) hut   b) door
   c) window   d) building

2. **The _____ dances gracefully.**
   a) singer   b) musician
   c) dancer   d) gymnast

3. **A tree has many _____.**
   a) leaves   b) bark
   c) trunk   d) roots

4. **A _____ sails on the sea.**
   a) ship   b) boat
   c) plane   d) car

5. He is carrying a _____ of water.
   a) tumbler   b) bottle

   c) bucket   d) drum

6. You wear a _____ when you go to school.
   a) perfume   b) uniform

   c) flower   d) skin

7. I breathe through my _____.
   a) neck   b) hands

   c) nose   d) ears

8. A _____ fights fire.
   a) fireman   b) policeman

   c) actor   d) politician

9. The young one of a cat is called a _____.
   a) cub   b) calf

   c) puppy   d) kitten

10. Sheena is learning to play the _____.
    a) guitar   b) drums

    c) violin   d) postman

Word Pairs/Odd One Out

Word Pairs

Look at the following:
Doors and windows
Shoes and socks
These are called **word pairs**.

EXERCISE 1

Choose the correct options to make proper word pairs.

1. Hands and _____ (legs/kidneys/hair)
2. Ladies and _____ (gentlemen/men/women)
3. Nephews and _____ (aunts/uncles/nieces)
4. Fruits and _____ (flowers/vegetables/water)
5. Sons and _____ (daughters/nieces/mothers)
6. Husband and _____ (woman/lady/wife)
7. Gold and _____ (platinum/diamond/silver)
8. Bread and _____ (cheese/butter/bowl)
9. Needle and _____ (thread/fork/knife)
10. Shirts and _____ (socks/trousers/shoes)

Odd One Out

Anything that does not belong to a group of similar things is considered to be an odd one out.

For example:

pigeon, sparrow, parrot, lion

Here, **lion** is the odd one out.

EXERCISE 2

Put a cross (X) against the odd one out.

1. a) sweater   b) coat
   c) shawl   d) T-shirt

2. a) fridge   b) table
   c) drawer   d) chair

3. a) Monday   b) Tuesday
   c) March   d) Sunday

4. a) notebook   b) book
   c) lunch box   d) diary

5. a) lady   b) gentleman
   c) girl   d) woman

6. a) Republic Day   b) Gandhi Jayanti
   c) Independence Day   d) Easter

7. a) tennis   b) badminton

    c) table tennis   d) football

8. a) violin   b) guitar

    c) hammer   d) sitar

9. a) apple   b) banana

    c) orange   d) cauliflower

10. a) movie   b) actor

    c) director   d) policeman

Words and Their Meanings

Ask your teacher for a book called **dictionary**. A dictionary has meanings of different words.

Some words have only one meaning. Some have more than one meaning. Every word has to have a meaning.

Let's practise the exercises given in this chapter. You may seek help from a dictionary if you are not sure of a word's meaning.

EXERCISE 1

Tick (✓) the correct meanings of the words given below.

1. **Near**
   a) close by   b) at a distance
   c) hot   d) quickly

2. **Glad**
   a) frightened   b) sad
   c) bad   d) happy

3. **Care**
   a) look after   b) press
   c) terror   d) move

4. **Frightened**

   a) stop b) ugly

   c) slowed down d) horrified

5. **Toes**

   a) car parts b) body parts

   c) something you use in the kitchen d) on the head

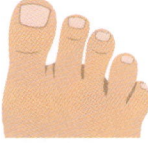

6. **Fresh**

   a) amazed b) new

   c) surprise d) happy

7. **Teacher**

   a) someone you meet in the hospital b) family member

   c) someone you learn from in school d) nursing assistant

8. **Postman**

   a) one who delivers letters b) family member

   c) someone you meet in the hospital d) nursing assistant

9. **Ambulance**

   a) takes you to the hospital b) racing car

   c) someone you meet in the post office d) theatre

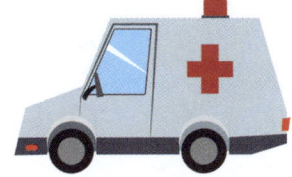

10. **Eyes**

    a) you see with them b) helps you hear

    c) helps you jump and play d) part of the toolkit

EXERCISE 2

Nisha is going to her school. Today in school, she would have to write the meanings of the following words. Can you help her write the meanings of the given words? You may take help from the words given in the box.

wise	shouting	to go out from
good looking	break	to take your time
silently	walk	
rush	an equipment used to put an end to fir	

Words   **Meanings**

1. Exit   _____
2. Intelligent   _____
3. Beautiful   _____
4. Screaming   _____
5. Fire extinguisher _____
6. Quietly   _____
7. Stroll   _____
8. Recess   _____
9. Haste   _____
10. Patience   _____

Opposites

Look at the words below.

Hot - Cold
Fast - Slow

These words are completely different from each other. As a pair, these are reverse of each other. Such pairs of words are called **opposites**.

Now let's practise the exercises given below:

EXERCISE 1

Match the following words with their opposites.

1.	Good	Dirty
2.	Cheap	Bad
3.	Clean	Open
4.	Light	Beautiful
5.	Ugly	Far
6.	Close	Late
7.	Near	Single
8.	Early	Active
9.	Pair	Expensive
10.	Lazy	Dark

EXERCISE 2

Rohan and Alisha are siblings. Rohan is **fat** while Alisha is **slim**. The words **fat** and **slim** are opposites of each other.

Choose the correct opposites from the brackets and write in the given spaces.

1. Happy   _____ (Ugly/Bad/Sad)

2. Careless   _____ (Careful/Open/Close)

3. Strong   _____ (Weak/Broken/Tough)

4. Hardworking   _____ (Young/Old/Lazy)

5. Funny   _____ (Boring/Caring/Casual)

6. Naughty   _____ (Funny/Dull/Old)

7. Thin   _____ (Short/Bloated/Fat)

8. Tall   _____ (Short/Thin/Long)

9. Cheerful   _____ (Gloomy/Happy/Dark)

10. Truthful   _____ (Liar/Honest/Caring)

Nouns

A **noun** is a naming word for a person, place or a thing.

For example:

Sachin, Sheena, New Delhi, India, etc.

EXERCISE 1

Which of these words of a sentence is a noun? Tick (✓) the correct answer in each of the following.

1. **Please open the door.**
   - a) Please
   - b) open
   - c) the
   - d) door

2. **Koel dances gracefully.**
   - a) Koel
   - b) dances
   - c) gracefully
   - d) the whole sentence

3. **Is that Rohan's car?**
   - a) Rohan and car
   - b) only Rohan
   - c) only car
   - d) that

4. **He is Dr Reddy.**
   - a) going
   - b) doctor
   - c) walk
   - d) Dr Reddy

5. Shaila opened all the windows of the classroom.
   a) Shaila, windows and classroom
   b) the
   c) opened
   d) all and the

6. They are running.
   a) They
   b) none of these
   c) are
   d) running

7. Where is your father?
   a) where
   b) is
   c) your
   d) father

8. Lions are dangerous.
   a) dangerous
   b) Lions
   c) are
   d) none of these

9. Paris is located in Europe.
   a) only Paris
   b) only Europe
   c) Paris and Europe
   d) located

10. Karan wears only Liberty shoes.
   a) Karan, Liberty and shoes
   b) Karan and shoes
   c) Karan and Liberty
   d) the whole sentence

Common Nouns

General names of people, places or things are common nouns.

For example:
boy, girl or table. A common noun does not begin with a capital letter, unless it comes in the beginning of the sentence.

| Boy | Girl | Table |

Proper Nouns

Names of specific persons, places or things are proper nouns.

For example:
Peter, Gateway of India, Eiffel Tower, etc.

| Peter | Gateway of India | Eiffel Tower |

EXERCISE 2

Write either proper noun or common noun against each of these words.

1. St Paul's Cathedral _____

2. Teacher _____

3. Statue of Liberty _____

4. Playground _____

5. Sydney Opera House _____

6. The Great Wall of China _____

7. Policeman _____

8. Racing Car _____

9. Barack Obama _____

10. Cell Phone _____

One and Many

Look at the following objects.

One book

Many books

One toy

Many toys

A single noun (book or toy) counted as one is written as it is. When there is more than one noun (books or toys), then we add **s** or **es**.

EXERCISE 1

Look at the words given below and write one or many.

1. Chalk _____ (one/many)
2. Benches _____ (one/many)
3. Flowers _____ (one/many)
4. Phone _____ (one/many)
5. Trees _____ (one/many)
6. Boat _____ (one/many)
7. Glass _____ (one/many)
8. Computers _____ (one/many)
9. Tiger _____ (one/many)
10. Bird _____ (one/many)

EXERCISE 2

Tick (✓) the correct plurals in each of the following.

1. **Poem**
   a) poemes   b) poems

2. **Pearl**
   a) pearls   b) pearles

3. **Village**
   a) villages   b) villags

4. **Egg**
    a) egges   b) eggs

5. **Room**
    a) rooms   b) roomes

6. **Town**
    a) townes   b) towns

7. **Story**
    a) storys   b) stories

8. **Thief**
    a) thieves   b) thiefs

9. **Judge**
    a) judges   b) judgees

10. **Board**
    a) boards   b) boardes

Gender

The state of being a male or a female is called **gender**.

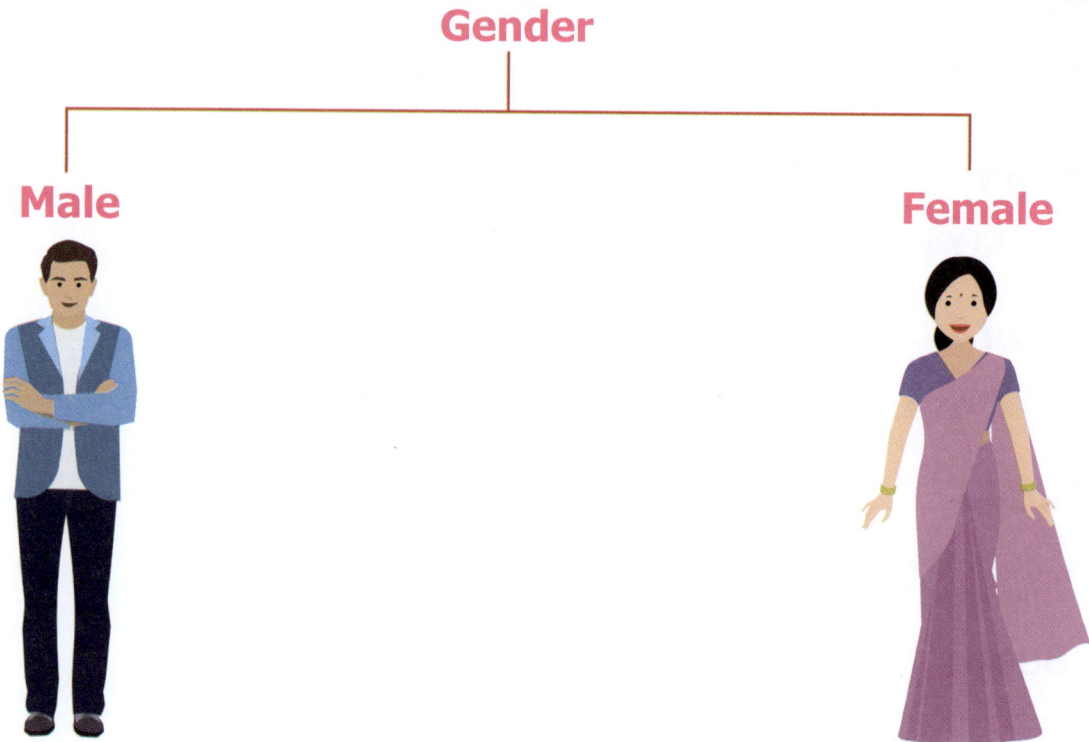

Nouns related to male gender are called **masculine**.

For example:
boy and man.

Nouns related to female gender are called **feminine**.

For example:
girl and woman.

Some nouns are common gender nouns. They are common to both the male and the female.

For example:
teacher and doctor.

EXERCISE 1

Tick (✓) the correct gender.

1. **Tiger**
   a) masculine　　　　　　　　　b) feminine
   c) common　　　　　　　　　　d) none of these

2. **Horse**
   a) masculine　　　　　　　　　b) feminine
   c) common　　　　　　　　　　d) none of these

3. **Astronaut**
   a) masculine　　　　　　　　　b) feminine
   c) common　　　　　　　　　　d) none of these

4. **Judge**
   a) masculine　　　　　　　　　b) feminine
   c) common　　　　　　　　　　d) none of these

5. **Doe**
   a) masculine　　　　　　　　　b) feminine
   c) common　　　　　　　　　　d) none of these

6. **Cow**
   a) masculine　　　　　　　　　b) feminine
   c) common　　　　　　　　　　d) none of these

7. **Grammar**
   a) masculine	b) feminine
   c) common	d) none of these

8. **Athlete**
   a) masculine	b) feminine
   c) common	d) none of these

9. **Madam**
   a) masculine	b) feminine
   c) common	d) none of these

10. **Nun**
    a) masculine	b) feminine
    c) common	d) none of these

EXERCISE 2

Choose the correct opposite gender.

1. **Bull**
   a) cow	b) cattle
   c) yak	d) none of these

2. **Mare**
   a) lad	b) lass
   c) donkey	d) horse

3. **Gentleman**
   a) man	b) girl
   c) lady	d) lad

4. Tiger

a) tigress   b) panther

c) lioness   d) none of these

5. Nephew

a) son   b) daughter

c) niece   d) grandson

6. Girl

a) boy   b) son

c) brat   d) nephew

7. Fox

a) jackal   b) he-fox

c) vixen   d) she-fox

8. Bridegroom

a) groom   b) hero

c) bride   d) heroine

9. Gander

a) goose   b) geese

c) duck   d) drake

10. Billy-goat

a) nanny-goat   b) he-goat

c) she-goat   d) none of these

PRONOUNS

Pronoun is a word that can be used in place of a noun - people, places and things.

For example:

Meher is a good girl.
Meher studies hard.

To avoid repeating **Meher** in the second sentence, we can rewrite it as:

Meher is a good girl.
She studies very hard.

I, she, he, you, we, they, it, etc. are pronouns.

EXERCISE 1

Tick (✓) the correct options.

1. **Which of these is a pronoun?**
   a) they   b) happy
   c) Nancy   d) none of these

2. **Which pronoun can replace the noun, Sheena?**
   a) he   b) she
   c) it   d) they

3. **Which of these is not a pronoun?**
   a) you   b) I
   c) child   d) it

4. **The tiger is in a zoo. Which pronoun can replace the words tiger and zoo?**
   a) it
   b) she
   c) he
   d) none of these

5. **Hyderabad is a city. _____ is the capital of two states.**
   a) It
   b) Her
   c) She
   d) It's

6. **_____ is a good doctor.**
   a) He or She
   b) It or They
   c) You
   d) Your

7. **Which of these can be replaced by a pronoun?**
   a) doing
   b) running
   c) fox
   d) working

8. **Which of these cannot be replaced by a pronoun?**
   a) close
   b) the workers
   c) the bride
   d) the heroine

9. **Sheena is an intelligent girl. Which of the words in the sentence is a pronoun?**
   a) Sheena
   b) girl
   c) none of these
   d) intelligent

10. **I went to see a movie yesterday. Which of the words in the sentence is a pronoun?**

   a) I

   b) movie

   c) yesterday

   d) went

EXERCISE 2

Fill in the blanks with the pronouns given in the choices.

1. **Nancy is a caring sister. _____ looks after her brother well.**

   a) He

   b) She

   c) Nancy

   d) It

2. **Sheena is in the girls' football team. _____ is a good team to be in.**

   a) He

   b) She

   c) It

   d) They

3. **The zookeeper is a watchful man. _____ does not let visitors cross the line.**

   a) He

   b) It

   c) The zookeeper

   d) They

4. **He gave me some chocolates, and _____ ate them there itself.**

   a) it

   b) I

   c) she

   d) none of these

5. _____ is a sensible thing to be alert.

   a) He b) It

   c) She d) It's

6. _____ is working hard to become a scientist.

   a) He or She b) It

   c) You d) Your

7. Rahul's mother is a teacher. _____ also teaches ____ at home.

   a) He and her b) She and her

   c) She and him d) He and she

8. All the boys beat up the thief. _____ did not show any mercy.

   a) They b) He

   c) She d) The boys

9. Helen does _____ homework herself. _____ does not need help.

   a) her, She b) girl, Boy

   c) none of these d) she, He

10. _____ wanted to enjoy myself.

    a) I b) They

    c) She d) He

Using A, An and The

In English alphabet, letters **a, e, i, o** and **u** are **vowels**. The remaining 21 letters are **consonants**.

Before the words beginning with vowels, consonants and specific nouns, we use **a, an** and **the** which are called articles.

A or **An** are used to show one out of many nouns.

For example:
a school means any school, but **the school** means a specific school.

We use **a** before the words beginning with consonant sounds.

For example:
a phone, **a** hat, **a** tiger.

We use **an** before the words beginning with vowels.

For example:
an apple, **an** umbrella, **an** insect.

EXERCISE 1

Fill in the blanks with the correct articles.

1. Mr. Narendra Modi is _____ Prime Minister of India. (a/an/the)

2. Who is _____ principal of your school? (a/an/the)

3. _____ apple a day, keeps the doctor away. (A/An/The)

4. Soubir wore _____ T-shirt to school. (a/an/the)

5. Shahrukh Khan is ____ actor. (a/an/the)

6. She is _____ officer in the Indian Air Force. (a/an/the)

7. Dr Hamid Ansari is _____ Vice President of India. (a/an/the)

8. He broke _____ buttons of his shirt. (a/an/the)

9. One must remain calm in _____ situation like this. (a/an/the)

10. I saw _____ elephant in the zoo. (a/an/the)

EXERCISE 2

Tick (✓) the correct options and fill in the blanks.

1. **Only _____ child can use this toy.**
   a) a
   b) an
   c) the
   d) none of these

2. **Kuwait is _____ good city.**
   a) a
   b) an
   c) the
   d) none of these

3. **_____ friend in need is a friend indeed.**
   a) A
   b) An
   c) The
   d) none of these

4. Who is at _____ door?

a) a b) an

c) the d) none of these

5. Call me only if there is _____ need.

a) a b) an

c) the d) none of these

6. Saina Nehwal is _____ badminton champion.

a) a b) an

c) the d) none of these

7. _____ pencil in your hand is not sharpened.

a) A b) An

c) The d) none of these

8. He is _____ amazing person.

a) a b) an

c) the d) none of these

9. Helen is _____ intelligent girl.

a) a b) an

c) the d) none of these

10. _____ Mr Atwal paints well.

a) a b) an

c) the d) none of these

Action Words

A word that shows an action or something being done is called an **action word**.

Walk, **play** or **run** are action words.

Let us use these in sentences to understand them better.

I **walk** slowly.

I **play** football.

I **run** fast.

EXERCISE 1

Which of these words are action words? Tick (✓) the correct options.

1.   a) sweater   b) wool

     c) knit   d) none of these

2.   a) window   b) slow

     c) wind   d) blow

3.   a) dance   b) gracefully

     c) she   d) all

4. a) calendar　　　　　　　　　b) year

    c) day　　　　　　　　　　　　d) none of these

5. a) school　　　　　　　　　　b) homework

    c) write　　　　　　　　　　　d) none of these

6. a) hoist　　　　　　　　　　　b) flag

    c) Independence Day　　　　　d) none of these

7. a) play　　　　　　　　　　　b) piano

    c) melody　　　　　　　　　　d) tunes

8. a) tennis　　　　　　　　　　b) championship

    c) team　　　　　　　　　　　d) none of these

9. a) apple　　　　　　　　　　　b) pie

    c) bake　　　　　　　　　　　d) none of these

10. a) cartoon　　　　　　　　　b) TV

    c) watch　　　　　　　　　　d) show

EXERCISE 2

Choose the correct action words and fill in the blanks.

1. I like to _____ video games. **(play/watch/jump)**

2. I _____ in a pool. **(run/swim/jump)**

3. The wind has _____ over the ocean. **(blown/jumped/run)**

4. She _____ delicious food. **(tasty/bakes/cooks)**

5. Let me _____ the door. **(open/jump/run)**

6. The horse _____ every morning. **(neighs/shouts/crawls)**

7. The spider _____ up the wall. **(crawls/gallops/runs)**

8. The lion _____ loudly. **(bleats/roars/talks)**

9. We _____ through the nose. **(smell/see/hear)**

10. I can _____ the drums well. **(play/throw/roll)**

PREPOSITIONS

12

A word used before a noun or pronoun and expressing a relation to another word is called a **preposition**.

For example:
The glass is **on** the table.

The cat is **under** the table.

EXERCISE 1

Look at the pictures and choose the correct options to fill in the blanks.

1. The girl is sitting _____ the boy.
   (behind/on/after)

2. The teacher is writing _____ the green board.
   (on/under/behind)

3. The dog is playing _____ the table.
   (on/under/across)

4. The car is running _____ the trucks.
   (over/between/below)

5. The girl is playing _____ the doll.
   (with/between/across)

6. He is standing _____ the house.
   (behind/across/in front of)

7. The horse jumped _____ the fence.
   (over/under/below)

8. The girl is standing _____ the road.
   (over/behind/across)

9. The post office is _____ the police station.
   (near/far/across)

10. Who is singing _____ the bathroom?
    (near/in/on)

EXERCISE 2

Tick (✓) the correct prepositions and fill in the blanks.

1. **Who is going to dinner _____ Friday?**
   a) on					b) for
   c) to					d) in

2. **Dinner is served _____ the table.**
   a) in					b) under the
   c) on					d) between

3. **The snake is hiding _____ the bushes.**
    a) in b) on
    c) over d) of

4. **He will call _____ 10.30 am.**
    a) at b) behind
    c) over d) between

5. **Let me bake a cake _____ Seher.**
    a) over b) to
    c) between d) for

6. **Let me play a game _____ you.**
    a) in b) at
    c) with d) over

7. **He visited us _____ dinner yesterday.**
    a) over b) below
    c) under d) in

8. **We care _____ each other.**
    a) for b) with
    c) under d) to

9. **He is sitting _____ the railway tracks.**
    a) in b) between
    c) for d) to

Describing Words

Look at the following examples.

A **beautiful** girl.

A **fat** hen.

The words **beautiful** and **fat** tell us something about the girl and hen. Such words are called **describing words**.

EXERCISE 1

Which of these is not a describing word? Put a cross (X) against the answer.

1. a) trouser   b) cold
   c) freezing   d) cool

2. a) window   b) slow
   c) windy   d) fast

3. a) singer   b) melodious
   c) soothing   d) good

4. a) fast   b) run
   c) slow   d) amazing

5. a) quiet   b) noisy
   c) classroom   d) soft-spoken

6. a) caring   b) deserving
    c) happy   d) God

7. a) beautiful   b) lovely
    c) wonderful   d) lady

8. a) high   b) huge
    c) big   d) mountain

9. a) tasty   b) delicious
    c) food   d) fantastic

10. a) ugly   b) sharp
    c) sad   d) movie

EXERCISE 2

Fill in the blanks with the correct describing words.

1. **It is a _____ day today.**
   a) sunny   b) first
   c) last   d) none of these

2. **Mrs Poonawala is an _____ woman.**
   a) lady   b) intelligent
   c) girl   d) none of these

3. **It was a _____ play.**
   a) enjoyed   b) good
   c) drama   d) stage

4. **It has been a _____ year.**
   a) wonderful
   b) month
   c) January
   d) day

5. **The rose smells very _____.**
   a) flower
   b) sweet
   c) petal
   d) none of these

6. **That is a _____ bird.**
   a) ostrich
   b) sparrow
   c) parrot
   d) none of these

7. **Mt. Everest is the _____ peak in the world.**
   a) highest
   b) deepest
   c) mountain
   d) none of these

8. **The Nile is the _____ river in the world.**
   a) happiest
   b) saddest
   c) longest
   d) none of these

9. **Mango is a _____ fruit.**
   a) delicious
   b) quiet
   c) happy
   d) none of these

10. **I watch an_____ shows on the television.**
    a) interesting
    b) radio
    c) like
    d) none of these

People and Professions/ Young Ones

EXERCISE 1

Tick (✓) the correct options.

1. He stitches clothes.
   a) tailor b) doctor
   c) policeman d) scientist

2. He makes things out of wood.
   a) carpenter b) blacksmith
   c) goldsmith d) none of these

3. He cures us when we are ill.
   a) doctor b) scientist
   c) curator d) lab assistant

4. He directs plays and movies.
   a) producer b) artist
   c) director d) actress

5. She acts in films and movies
   a) artist b) actress
   c) director d) none of these

6. **He mends our shoes.**
   a) postman
   b) cobbler
   c) watchman
   d) none

7. **He guards our houses at night.**
   a) watchman
   b) policeman
   c) doctor
   d) scientist

8. **He fights with enemies at the border and protects the country.**
   a) policeman
   b) watchman
   c) soldier
   d) none of these

9. **He flies a plane.**
   a) pilot
   b) driver
   c) sailor
   d) none of these

10. **He or she draws and paints.**
    a) writer
    b) actress
    c) pilot
    d) artist

EXERCISE 2

Choose and write the young ones for the following.

1. Tiger _____ (cub/calf/kitten)

2. Cat _____ (cub/calf/kitten)

3. Dog _____ (cub/calf/puppy)

4. Cow _____ (foal/calf/kitten)

5. Deer _____ (cub/fawn/puppy)

6. Horse _____ (foal/calf/duckling)

7. Lion _____ (cub/calf/kitten)

8. Bear _____ (cub/calf/puppy)

9. Sheep _____ (foal/lamb/piglet)

10. Duck _____ (duckling/chick/lamb)

COMPREHENSION

Passage

Read the passage given below and fill in the blanks with the correct options.

Sheetal is a good girl. She studies hard and is also good in sports. Like her father, she wants to become a doctor when she grows up. Her father helps her in her studies after he returns home from work. Her teachers are very proud of her.

1. Sheetal is good in _____.
   (studies and sports/music)

2. Sheetal's father is a _____.
   (engineer/doctor/policeman)

3. He helps Sheetal in her _____.
   (studies/games/school activities)

4. Sheetal makes her _____ proud.
   (parents/happy/teachers)

5. We can say that Sheetal is a _____ girl.
   (responsible/bad/terrible)

EXERCISE 2

Poem

Read the poem below and tick the correct options.

Chatterford Market (An Extract)

Cabbage and carrots,

Beetroot and beans,

Spinach and sprouts,

Marrows and greens:

All of the freshest

Crispy and spry,

At Chatterford Market,

Buy! Come buy!
- Paul King

1. **What is the name of the market?**

    a) Chatterford   b) Indian

    c) Oxford   d) Fish Market

2. **What is being sold at the market?**

    a) vegetables   b) fruits

    c) spoons   d) nothing

3. **Which of these is not available in the market?**
   a) spinach b) mangoes
   c) beans d) beetroot

4. **Can you buy some sprouts in the market?**
   a) Yes b) No

5. **Are all the things sold crisp and fresh?**
   a) Yes b) No

EXERCISE 3

Speaking and Writing

Choose the correct answers.

1. **How will you seek permission to enter a classroom?**
   a) Can I go in?
   b) May I come in, please?
   c) I am coming in.
   d) None of these

2. **What would you say to your friend if you were to borrow an eraser?**
   a) Can I borrow your eraser?
   b) Might I borrow your eraser?
   c) Could I borrow your eraser, please?
   d) I am taking your eraser.

Now, choose a reply for the following questions.

3. **May I borrow your stationery?**

    a) Yes, you may.

    b) Yes, you can.

    c) Take it.

    d) No, not at all.

4. **Thank you for inviting me to your birthday party.**

    a) You are welcome!

    b) It's alright!

    c) Never mind!

    d) Ok!

5. **What would you say if you were to leave the classroom?**

    a) May I please leave the classroom?

    b) I am leaving the class.

    c) May I please go?

    d) Thank you, I had a nice day.

Model Test Paper-I

Choose the correct words from the brackets and fill in the blanks.

1. _____ weather is bad today. (A/An/The)

2. We must _____ a good game. (throw/play/hoist)

3. Rahul is a _____ chess player. (good/intelligent/sad)

4. _____ is a sad today. (It/They/He)

5. _____ all the boxes to find the keys. (Close/Open/Blast)

6. We must play a match _____ them. (to/of/with)

7. Mary had _____ little lamb. (a/an/the)

8. She was _____ badly. (celebrated/hurt/praised)

9. Please guide _____ to the men's bathroom. (her/him/she)

10. Mr Alexander _____ paintings. (makes/throws/howls)

Choose the odd one out.

11. a) cream   b) oil

    c) powder   d) chalk

12. a) Tom and Jerry   b) Ben 10

    c) Mickey Mouse   d) Rose

13. a) television   b) fridge

    c) couch   d) iron

14. a) sand   b) branches

    c) root   d) leaves

15. a) river   b) ocean

    c) sea   d) swimming pool

Identify the pictures and then tick (✓) the correct options.

16. a) basket   b) bucket

    c) pram   d) drum

17. a) latch   b) window

    c) door   d) gate

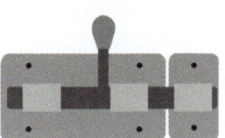

18. a) television   b) radio

    c) CD player   d) laptop

19. a) eggs   b) chicken

    c) chocolates   d) honey

20. a) fingers   b) hair

    c) hands   d) toes

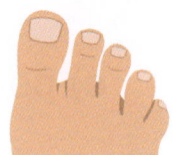

Choose the correct options and fill in the blanks.

21. Young one of a dog is called a _____. (kitten/calf/puppy)

22. The word 'purse' is a _____
    (preposition/common noun/describing word)

23. The _____ is dressing the wound on his knee.
    (nurse/operator/receptionist)

24. Mrs Sharma _____ maths in Rohan's school.
    (cures/teaches/plays)

25. The opposite of wet is _____. (damp/cloudy/dry)

26. The meaning of evil is _____. (kill/die/bad)

27. 'Dive' is an _____. (describing word/noun/action word)

28. Rahul is climbing on the roof of his house in the rain - 'the' used twice in this sentence is an _____.
    (preposition/article/common noun)

29. The masculine gender of waitress is called _____.
    (waiter/chef/nurse)

30. What word can you make by rearranging the jumbled letters useppr? _____ (supper/usurp/super)

MODEL TEST PAPER-2

Choose the correct words from the brackets and fill in the blanks.

1. When a person has to fight a case in court, he goes to a _____.
   (doctor/lawyer/plumber)

2. A table can be paired with a _____. (horse/almirah/chair)

3. Horses _____. (walk/fly/gallop)

4. Let us be _____ to watch the play. (seated/watched/spoken)

5. Our country's name is India. India is a _____.
   (proper noun/describing word/action word)

6. The odd one out among sparrow, crow, pigeon and whale is_____. (sparrow/crow/pigeon/whale)

7. The sun _____ in the east. (rises/sets/drowns)

8. I can see an airplane in _____ sky. (my/a/the)

9. Vixen is the feminine gender of _____. (ox/fox/hare)

10. A cobbler _____ shoes. (cares/mends/hosts)

Read the following poem and fill in the blanks.

Cats sleep anywhere, any table, any chair,

Top of piano, window-ledge, in the middle, on the edge,

Open draw, empty shoe, anybody's lap will do,

Fitted in a cardboard box, in the cupboard with your frocks,

Anywhere! They don't care! Cats sleep anywhere.

— By Eleanor Farjeon

11. This poem is about _____. (cats/cardboard boxes/pianos)

12. Cats can sleep _____ the piano. (under/inside/on top of)

13. For them to sleep, the shoe has to be _____.
(closed/empty/full)

14. They can sleep with frocks in the _____.
(cardboard box/shoe/cupboard)

15. Do cats care? _____ (No/Yes)

Match the following.

16. Buds	Flower
17. Parents	Pairs
18. Flowers	Butterflies
19. Butterfly	Bud
20. Pair	Parent

Choose the correct options for the highlighted words.

21. **Dr Kalam** was the President of India.

   a) common noun   b) proper noun

   c) name of a profession   d) none of these

22. Megha will be travelling to the South **with** her parents.

   a) preposition   b) article

   c) common noun   d) all of these

Choose the correct options.

23. More than one lice is called:

   a) louse   b) blouse

   c) mouse   c) house

24. What does the word 'brave' mean?

   a) fearless   b) high

   c) coward   d) none of these

25. What does the word 'true' mean?

   a) lie   b) talk

   c) false   d) none of these

26. What is the opposite of 'young'?

   a) child
   b) youth
   c) old
   d) all of these

27. The masculine gender of 'authoress' is:

   a) writer
   b) author
   c) lawyer
   d) novelist

28. The young one of a swan is called:

   a) foal
   b) piglet
   c) cygnet
   d) none of these

29. Rearrange the letters LKIE to make a word:

   a) KILE
   b) KELI
   c) IKEL
   d) LIKE

30. The masculine gender for 'mayoress' is:

   a) mayor
   b) author
   c) maid
   d) none of these

Model Test Paper-3

Choose the correct options to make pairs.

1. Wheels and _____ (bicycles/tyres/cars)

2. Radio and _____ (television/mobile/ipad)

3. An arm and a _____ (hand/fingers/leg)

4. Law and _____ (order/public/politicians)

5. Government and _____ (police/servants/citizens)

Choose the correct options.

6. Who amongst these would run in a race? _____.
   (pilot/clown/athlete)

7. A pair of socks can be paired with a pair of _____.
   (trousers/gloves/shoes)

8. Pigeons _____. (gallop/fly/trot)

9. Drinking water must not be _____. (wasted/drunk/served)

10. Walking, drinking and eating are _____
    (proper nouns/describing words/action words)

11. Which is the odd one out - movie screen, seats, popcorn or bed? _____

12. Rearrange the letters to make a word - NIABC. _____

13. We must _____ each other. (hit/fight with/help)

14. Girl is the feminine gender of _____. (man/woman/boy)

15. A _____ steals cars. (burglar/postman/thief)

16. Asleep is the opposite of _____. (slept/awake/action)

17. The meaning of quick is to be _____. (happy/asleep/fast)

18. If I am seated in a car, I am being driven by a _____.
    (pilot/driver/sailor)

19. If I have to buy groceries, I would go to a _____.
    (shopkeeper/storekeeper/grocer)

20. A barber cuts our _____. (legs/hair/teeth)

Choose and write the correct nouns for the action words.

21. eat   _____   (food/insects/stomach)

22. drink   _____   (food/water/soil)

23. listen   _____   (park/music/cars)

24. hit   _____   (ball/airplane/food)

25. fly   _____   (car/helicopter/truck)

Choose the correct describing words for the nouns.

26. delicious _____ (animal/meal/water)

27. slow _____ (tortoise/hare/tiger)

28. fast _____ (tortoise/athlete/river)

29. high _____ (cow/buffalo/mountain)

30. low _____ (man/plains/clouds)

Answer Key

Chapter 1
Exercise 1

1. d
2. c
3. b
4. b
5. a
6. c
7. d
8. a
9. b
10. c

Exercise 2

1. b
2. c
3. a
4. b
5. c
6. a
7. b
8. c
9. a
10. d

Chapter 2
Exercise 1

1. a
2. d
3. c
4. a
5. d
6. b
7. b
8. a
9. a
10. c

Exercise 2

1. a
2. c
3. a

4. a
5. b
6. b

7. c
8. a
9. d

10. c

Chapter 3
Exercise 1

1. legs
2. gentlemen
3. nieces

4. vegetables
5. daughters
6. wife

7. silver
8. butter
9. thread

10. trousers

Exercise 2

1. d
2. a
3. c

4. c
5. b
6. d

7. d
8. c
9. d

10. d

Chapter 4
Exercise 1

1. a
2. d
3. a

4. d　　　　　　　　5. b　　　　　　　　6. b

7. c　　　　　　　　8. a　　　　　　　　9. a

10. a

Exercise 2

1. to go out from　　2. wise　　　　　　3. good looking

4. shouting　　　　　5. an equipment used to put an end to fire

6. silently　　　　　7. walk　　　　　　8. break

9. rush　　　　　　　10. to take your time

Chapter 5
Exercise 1

1. Good - Bad　　　　2. Cheap - Expensive

3. Clean - Dirty　　　4. Light - Dark

5. Ugly - Beautiful　　6. Close - Open

7. Near - Far　　　　8. Early - Late

9. Pair - Single　　　10. Lazy - Active

Exercise 2

1. Happy　　　　　　Sad

2. Careless　　　　　Careful

3.	Strong	Weak
4.	Hardworking	Lazy
5.	Funny	Boring
6.	Naughty	Dull
7.	Thin	Fat
8.	Tall	Short
9.	Cheerful	Gloomy
10.	Truthful	Liar

Chapter 6
Exercise 1

1. d   2. a   3. a

4. d   5. a   6. b

7. d   8. b   9. c

10. a

Exercise 2

Proper Nouns: 1, 3, 5, 6; 9; Common Nouns: 2, 4, 7, 8, 10

Chapter 7
Exercise 1

1. one   2. many   3. many

4. one 5. many 6. one

7. one 8. many 9. one

10. one

Exercise 2

1. b 2. a 3. a

4. b 5. a 6. b

7. b 8. a 9. a

10. a

Chapter 8
Exercise 1

1. a 2. a 3. c

4. c 5. b 6. b

7. d 8. c 9. b

10. b

Exercise 2

1. a 2. d 3. c

4. a 5. c 6. a

7. c 8. c 9. a

10. a

Chapter 9
Exercise 1

1. a
2. b
3. c
4. a
5. a
6. a
7. c
8. a
9. c
10. a

Exercise 2

1. b
2. b
3. a
4. b
5. b
6. a
7. c
8. a
9. a
10. a

Chapter 10
Exercise 1

1. the
2. the
3. An
4. a
5. an
6. an
7. the
8. the
9. a
10. an

Exercise 2

1. a
2. a
3. a
4. c
5. a
6. a

7. c   8. b   9. b

10. d

Chapter 11
Exercise 1

1. c   2. d   3. a

4. d   5. c   6. a

7. a   8. d   9. c

10. c

Exercise 2

1. play   2. swim   3. blown

4. cooks   5. open   6. neighs

7. crawls 8. roars   9. smell

10. play

Chapter 12
Exercise 1

1. behind   2. on   3. under

4. between 5. with   6. in front of

7. over   8. across 9. near

10. in

69

Exercise 2

1. a	2. c	3. a
4. a	5. d	6. c
7. a	8. a	9. b

Chapter 13
Exercise 1

1. a	2. a	3. a
4. b	5. c	6. d
7. d	8. d	9. c
10. d		

Exercise 2

1. a	2. b	3. b
4. a	5. b	6. d
7. a	8. c	9. a
10. a		

Chapter 14
Exercise 1

| 1. a | 2. a | 3. a |
| 4. c | 5. b | 6. b |

7. a   8. c   9. a

10. d

Exercise 2

1. cub   2. kitten   3. puppy

4. calf   5. fawn   6. foal

7. cub   8. cub   9. lamb

10. duckling

Chapter 15
Exercise 1

1. studies and sports   2. doctor   3. studies

4. teachers   5. responsible

Exercise 2

1. a   2. c   3. b

4. a   5. a

Exercise 3

1. b   2. c   3. a

4. a   5. a

Model Test Paper-1

1. The 2. play 3. good 4. It 5. Open 6. with 7. a 8. hurt 9. him 10. makes 11. d 12. d 13. c 14. a 15. d 16. a 17. a 18. b 19. b 20. d 21. puppy 22. common noun 23. nurse 24. teaches 25. dry 26. bad 27. action word 28. article 29. waiter 30. supper.

Model Test Paper-2

1. lawyer 2. chair 3. gallop 4. seated 5. proper noun 6. whale 7. rises 8. the 9. fox 10. mends 11. cats 12. on top of 13. empty 14. cupboard 15. no 16. Bud 17. Parent 18. Flower 19. Butterflies 20. Pairs 21. b 22. a 23. a 24. a 25. d 26. c 27. b 28. c 29. d 30. a.

Model Test Paper-3

1. tyres 2. television 3. leg 4. order 5. citizens 6. athlete 7. shoes 8. fly 9. wasted 10. action words 11. bed 12. CABIN 13. help 14. boy 15. thief 16. awake 17. fast 18. driver 19. grocer 20. hair 21. food 22. water 23. music 24. ball 25. helicopter 26. meal 27. tortoise 28. athlete 29. mountain 30. plains.